TABLE OF CONTENTS

TABLE OF CONTENTS v

ACKNOWLEDGMENTS vii

FISCAL REALITY AFTER THE 2008 FINANCIAL CRISIS 1

Introduction 1

    The Crisis 1

    The Consequences 1

    Impact on the Army 3

Background 3

    Contributing Factors 3

        • Monetary Policy 4

        Housing Bubble 5

        Securitization and Financial Instruments 7

        Quantitative Financial Models 8

        Rating Agencies 9

        Deregulation and Oversight 10

        Financial Leverage 11

        Moral Hazard 12

        Systemic Risk 14

        Globalization 15

Analysis 16

    Government Response 17

    Deficit Spending and the National Debt 18

  The Danger 19

   A National Security Issue 20

 Reforming the System 22

  The Financial Sector 22

  The Military 23

Recommendations 26

 Financial Contingency Plans 26

 Army Financial Reform 27

 Educate the Workforce 31

Conclusion 32

BIBLIOGRAPHY 35

ENDNOTES 39

FISCAL REALITY AFTER THE 2008 FINANCIAL CRISIS

Introduction

The Crisis

The bursting of an unprecedented housing bubble in the US in late 2006 triggered the worldwide financial crisis of 2008. The end of this unsustainable rise in home prices caught most financial institutions completely off guard. As home prices fell in 2007 and 2008, mortgage defaults rose, causing the securities backed by those home loans to fall dramatically in value. Banks and financial institutions faced massive losses on the mortgage-backed securities that made up a large portion of the assets on their balance sheets. They resorted to selling their most liquid assets—shares of common stock—to raise funds to meet capital requirements and to stave off insolvency. The widespread sell off of stocks led to a precipitous drop in the stock markets and the panic in the financial sector caused the credit markets to freeze eliminating most sources of credit for consumers and businesses. The crisis in the US immediately spread across the globe because today's financial markets are tightly interwoven and because the securities backed by US mortgages had been purchased by financial entities in nearly every country. The calamity is now commonly referred to as the *Great Recession*.

The Consequences

The consequences of the financial crisis, the most severe since the Great Depression of the 1930s, were crippling here in the US and overseas. Home prices fell nationwide, an event that most economists and financial experts considered impossible. The worst hit areas in California, Nevada, and Florida saw drops of 50% or more. As prices slid, buyers were not able to refinance mortgages and millions went into default. Mortgage defaults destroyed the market for securities backed by home loans and the resulting losses crippled the financial sector. All five of the largest investment banks in the US went out of business, were bought out by another financial institution, or converted themselves to bank holding companies in order to survive. Numerous banks and other financial entities declared bankruptcy; this effect is still unfolding in early 2010.

The stock markets in the US dropped by more than 50% between October 2007 and March 2009, destroying trillions of dollars in wealth. Cash-strapped businesses laid off millions of employees, driving the unemployment rate to a high of 10.2% in late 2008. Those jobless Americans and many more worried about losing their jobs cut back on consumer spending creating a vicious cycle of declining prices and falling demand across the economy.

Finally, credit markets froze as banks and the other financial institutions that provided this essential resource for businesses and consumers saw their capital reserves depleted. The federal government was forced to step in to avoid a complete meltdown of America's financial sector. Hundreds of billions of taxpayer dollars were committed to bail out financial institutions, car companies, and the largest insurance company in the US. Additional measures were taken by the government to shore up the mortgage industry, assist homeowners with underwater mortgages, jumpstart the credit markets, and stimulate the creation of new jobs.

Impact on the Army

The key issue in the aftermath of the Great Recession is to determine if the crisis has changed the national security environment and to determine how any such changes will affect the US Army. This paper will examine the factors that led to the crisis, provide an analysis of those results of the crisis that can be related to the Army, and offer recommendations for the Army to pursue.

Background

Contributing Factors

What caused the worldwide financial crisis of 2008? This question is being hotly debated and will continue to be a topic of discussion for decades to come, just as the roots of the Great Depression of the 1930s continue to inspire argument today. Hundreds of books, journal articles, and newspaper pieces have been published in the last two years authored by economists, bankers, financial experts, and academics. The various schools of economic thought each espouse a line of reasoning that seeks to explain what went wrong in the American capitalist system. This lively debate will not be resolved here. Instead, ten of the most common contributing factors described by experts today will be outlined. In the current complex financial environment, all these factors worked together with each other to generate a perfect storm that brought the financial system to the brink of complete collapse. Many of the causes of the recent calamity are still at work in the background and only time will tell if a permanent recovery is taking place.

- **Monetary Policy**

The Federal Reserve Act of 1913 established the Federal Reserve System (traditionally referred to as *the Fed*) as the central banking system for the US. One of the Fed's main responsibilities is to set monetary policy for the nation, and it does so primarily by controlling the federal funds interest rate. This rate is the amount that banks charge each other for overnight loans of funds held in reserve at the Fed. The Fed moves this key interest rate up or down depending on prevailing economic conditions.

The Fed cut the federal funds rate dramatically starting in 2000 in response to the recession brought on by the bursting of the "dot com bubble" and the rate reached 1% in 2003. The rate remained at 1% until mid-2004 and was gradually increased to 5% in 2006. The argument for loose monetary policy as a cause of the 2008 financial crisis is that the Fed left the interest rate too low for too long and that the easy money fueled an unsustainable increase in home prices, which led to abuses in the mortgage markets, and enabled many Americans to refinance their mortgages too easily.

The Taylor Rule, developed by Professor John Taylor of Stanford University, calculates a preferred federal funds rate based on the inflation rate and the Gross Domestic Product (GDP). Use of this tool shows that the Fed did hold the federal funds rate below the expected level between 2004 and 2006.[1] The Fed chairman, Ben Bernanke, has disagreed publicly with the assertion that rates were kept artificially low. In a recent speech to the American Economic Association, he said, "Only a small portion of the increase in house prices earlier this decade can be attributed to stance of US monetary policy."[2] This debate is interesting in light of the current situation in which the federal funds rate has been lowered to a new low of 0.25% and is being maintained there for an extended period.

Housing Bubble

The financial environment has been marked by boom and bust cycles in many different asset classes throughout history. The asset class that triggered the financial crisis of 2008 was housing. Home prices in the US have trended upward over the decades at a rate just slightly higher than the rate of inflation. From 1997 to 2006, however, prices across the country increased an average of 85%. The markets in California, Nevada, and Florida saw much greater increases.[3] Why did home prices rocket upward beginning in 1997?

Many forces interacted to cause the boom starting in the 1990s and the bust in 2006. There was a general push to promote home ownership in the US and this led to a lowering of lending standards. The Federal National Mortgage Association (FNMA) and the Federal Home Loan Mortgage Corporation (FHLMC) are more commonly referred to as *Fannie Mae* and *Freddie Mac*. These Government-Sponsored Enterprises (GSEs) were established decades ago to purchase loans from banks and other financial entities that originate mortgages. By purchasing the mortgages, Fannie Mae and Freddie Mac assumed the risk of default on the home loans while allowing the originators to go out and make more loans.[4]

Fannie Mae and Freddie Mac began to reduce the credit requirements on the loans being purchased after receiving pressure from the Clinton Administration to provide more options for affordable housing especially for minorities and those with low incomes. There were attempts to tighten the regulation on these organizations in recognition that their loan portfolios were becoming more risky. However, the effort failed, default risk continued to build up, and in 2008, the federal government took over these monstrous GSEs.

Lending standards declined across the industry. The Community Reinvestment Act, passed by the Carter Administration and then reinvigorated under President Clinton, threatened financial institutions with lawsuits if they did not make enough loans to minorities. Banks and other mortgage originators reacted to all the government pressure by offering home loans to anyone who could sign their name.[5] Buyers who could not qualify for a prime loan could now get a sub-prime loan. Mortgages were offered with zero down, as interest only, or even as negative amortization loans. Payments on the latter did not even cover the monthly interest charges and the outstanding loan balance increased each month. Buyers who took out these exotic mortgages assumed, or were led to believe, that they would be able to refinance in a few years when their homes had appreciated in value.

As discussed previously, the Fed maintained low interest rates. Low interest rates allowed borrowers to purchase a home for the first time or to be able to purchase a larger home than would have been possible at higher rates. Additionally, the tax code in the US promotes home ownership due to the deductibility of mortgage interest. All the things that promoted home ownership pushed demand for homes upward. With so much money chasing too few homes, average home prices soared. While home values normally rise about 1% faster than inflation, from 2000 to 2006 the prices in major markets increased by more than 14% annually.[6] The home-building industry responded to increased demand by building more houses, thus setting the stage for the bust. Rising interest rates and too much inventory burst the housing bubble in late 2006, which triggered the financial crisis of 2008.

Securitization and Financial Instruments

The US financial industry is the most efficient at allocating capital and has led the world in developing innovative ways to do so. A key innovation was *securitization* and the creation of unique *financial instruments* designed to transfer or spread the inherent financial risk that is always present in financial markets. Almost anything that has a future stream of payments can be securitized, including mortgages, credit card balances, and student loans. In the old days, banks originated mortgages and kept all the home loans on their books, thereby assuming the risk of default on those loans. The originator today sells most mortgages to a firm that specializes in pooling the mortgages and packaging them into *mortgage-backed securities* (MBSs). The MBSs are sold to investors who receive a portion of the interest and principal from the underlying loans and now bear the risk of default on the loans. The main advantage of securitization is that it frees up the capital of the originators to make more loans.

In 2002, Fannie Mae, Freddie Mac, and the Federal Home Loan Bank (FHLB) controlled 73% of the mortgage securitization business. Due to the profitability of mortgage securities from the fees collected, private financial institutions entered the market to compete with the three GSEs and by 2006 were creating 56% of the new mortgage securities.[7] The types of mortgages being securitized are also important. In 2001, prime mortgages accounted for 86% of MBSs, but by 2006 this had fallen to 52%. Nearly half of the mortgages being converted to securities that year were from non-prime mortgages that were based on lower lending standards.[8]

Mortgage securitization contributed to the financial crisis in several ways. First, the attempt to spread the financial risk failed. The quantitative models that were behind many of the MBSs did not account for the remote possibility that a large number of homeowners would default on their payments simultaneously. Second, the rating agencies evaluating the securities prior to sale to investors gave the financial products ratings that were far too safe. Third, the near-universal belief that home prices would always go up caused financial institutions, institutional investors, and private individuals all to gorge on MBSs. The underlying risk was spread throughout the entire market, including overseas.

Quantitative Financial Models

A central theme in the recent financial crisis is the reliance on mathematical models. The financial innovation of MBSs was only the beginning as more exotic forms of MBSs followed. The MBSs were first cut into slices or *tranches*, with the tranches carrying different yields based on the risk of default of the underlying mortgages. A *collateralized debt obligation* (CDO) is a pool of these MBS tranches that is then cut into tranches and issued as securities. While the MBSs were backed by the payment flows from the underlying mortgages, the CDOs were one step removed from these cash flows.[9] Other financial instruments followed that were two or more steps removed from the original source of the cash flows.

Sophisticated math is also a key to creating *credit default swaps* (CDSs), a form of financial derivative. These instruments are designed as protection against the default on bonds or tranches of MBSs. Insurance companies or financial institutions issue CDSs to buyers who pay an *insurance* premium to the issuer. In return, the issuer agrees to pay the value of the bond to the buyer if it goes into default. From 2001 to 2007, the value of outstanding CDSs increased from $1 trillion to $60 trillion.[10]

Quantitative analysts—sometimes referred to as *quants*—which were employed in the financial sector, created these complex mathematical models. These quants were brilliant individuals, but their models turned out to be wrong in many cases. In hindsight, it can be seen that the models were too optimistic because they were based on recent trend lines that were strongly positive. The models for new financial instruments had little historical background on which to draw and did not take into account the possibility that seemingly unrelated events could actually be linked. Additionally, the financial incentives provided to the model creators biased them to make optimistic projections while many of the senior executives at financial firms did not understand how risk was being modeled in the calculations.[11]

Rating Agencies

As the quants were designing mathematical models that did not account for the financial risk, the rating agencies were using some of those same techniques to rate the bonds, MBSs, and other securities being marketed to investors. The three main rating agencies in the US are Moody's Corporation, Standard & Poor's, and Fitch, Inc. The Securities and Exchange Commission (SEC) oversees ratings agencies and, in 1975, established a new category called a *Nationally Recognized Statistical Rating Organization* (NRSRO) to let the financial markets know which agencies were preferred to deliver credit ratings on bonds.

The credit rating agencies received 90% of their revenues in 2000 from ratings fees paid by issuers of bonds and other securities. A corporate bond rating might generate up to $300,000, while a complex instrument like a MBS could yield up to $2 million. The three main agencies had total revenues in 2007 of $6 billion and profit margins that approached or exceeded 50%.[12] These large profits lead to the charge that the rating agencies have a conflict of interest, as they are receiving fees from the same firms that are expecting high ratings on the securities being designed for sale to investors. The rating agencies clearly failed to provide ratings that reflected the inherent risk in the financial products being rated prior to the financial crisis. In addition, the rating agencies have consulting arms that provide advice to issuers of securities on the best way to structure the instruments. Therefore, in at least some cases, they are rating the same products that they had a large part in designing. This is a clear conflict of interest.

Deregulation and Oversight

Another common cause cited for the financial crisis is *deregulation*, the idea that government systematically stripped away regulations designed to provide oversight to the financial sector or that the authorities failed to enact new legislation to control the financial innovations coming out of the industry. The thoughts of Henry Kaufman, a 26-year veteran of Salomon Brothers, which also operated as Salomon Smith Barney and is currently merged with Citigroup, and president of his own investment firm (Henry Kaufman and Co.) since 1988, are typical. He said at a 1987 symposium,

> Extraordinary changes are taking place in the financial markets, and Congress and regulators are slow in responding to these changes. Simply put, our financial system is going astray. Many deposit institutions are weak, and businesses and households have assumed massive debt burdens. This poses serious risks for our economy. In light of these risks, the current system of financial regulation is inadequate to deal with the changes in financial markets. Congress should abandon the current system and pass comprehensive legislation to install a better one.[13]

Others, particularly those who espouse free-market principles, disagree that lack of regulation was a reason for the crisis. They argue that the present financial system needs to be reformed by the market. Thomas E. Woods, Jr., a senior fellow with the Ludwig von Mises Institute in Alabama, says

> The problem, in short, is not "regulation" or the lack thereof. Once again, the problem is the system itself, a system that artificially encourages indebtedness, excessive leverage, and reckless money management in general. The money and banking system we have now, which is nearly as far removed from a genuine free market as it is possible to be, is so fragile and prone to instability that it's no wonder people call for more "regulation."[14]

There are numerous examples held up as evidence of deregulation as a cause of the financial crisis such as the repeal of the Glass Steagall Act in 1999. Many cases could be cited as evidence of failure to regulate financial innovations such as occurred throughout the 1990s when legislators held hearings, drafted proposed bills, but ultimately did not pass laws in Congress that would provide oversight of financial derivatives.[15]

Financial Leverage

A key argument made for deregulation or lack of regulation as a primary contributor to the financial crisis is that these factors led to excessive financial leverage being employed by financial institutions. *Financial leverage* for a corporation is simply the ratio of debt to equity or the ratio of borrowed assets to owned assets[16]—a fairly simple concept. If an investor has $100,000 to invest he could get a return of $10,000. To leverage the investment, he can borrow $500,000. Now he invests $600,000 and earns $60,000, a return of 60% at a leverage ratio of 6-to-1.[17] Thus, financial leverage is used to boost returns, particularly in environments where interest rates are low and investments are yielding low returns.

The catch is that a highly leveraged firm could incur significant losses in a market that drops only a small amount. In fact, financial leveraging tends to magnify losses more than it does gains. In 2006, many banks and financial institutions had borrowed heavily and had increased their financial leverage ratios to 30-to-1 or even higher. When the housing bubble exploded in late 2006, mortgage defaults rocketed upward, which caused MBSs to lose value. Financial firms that had borrowed heavily to invest in MBSs found that the assets on their balance sheets were no longer there. Financial leverage brought these companies to the brink of insolvency. Many that did not receive capital from the federal government went bankrupt.

Moral Hazard

Moral hazard is "…a term borrowed from the insurance business to describe the temptation to take bigger risks because someone else will pay the cost if things go wrong."[18] It results from the *too-big-to-fail* problem. The idea is that some financial institutions cannot be allowed to go bankrupt because they are so large and are so interconnected to other firms that their failure would endanger the entire financial system. If the government is willing to step in to prevent failure, the financial institutions will have an incentive to take on excess risk in order to increase their profits. In this way, the government guarantee against bankruptcy created a moral hazard.

Too-big-to-fail is a perception that built up over time. The federal government rescued Continental Illinois National Bank and Trust Company, based in Chicago, in

1984. Two months later, Todd Conover, the Comptroller of the Currency, informed Congress that the government would not allow any of the eleven largest banks to fail.[19] In 1998, the New York Federal Reserve brokered the rescue of the hedge fund Long-Term Capital Management (LTCM) due to the systemic risk that its ties posed to the rest of the financial system. As the financial crisis unfolded in 2008, too-big-to-fail came to another firm's aid. The nation's fifth largest investment banking company, Bear Stearns and Co., Inc., was rescued in March of that year. Later in 2008, the federal government took an 80% ownership stake in American International Group, Inc. (AIG), the largest insurance company in America.

A related issue to the too-big-to-fail problem is that of *too-big-to-manage*. As financial firms consolidated and grew in size, their organizational structures became excessively complex. This made it nearly impossible for senior executives to understand or control the amount of risk being taken in far-flung business operations. Lehman Brothers Holdings, Inc. went bankrupt in 2008 and financial experts are still trying to untangle the web of financial instruments and organizational structures of the company so that any remaining assets can be recovered and distributed to creditors. Also, many executives at large financial institutions did not have the knowledge to monitor the risk inherent in the new financial instruments being developed and marketed by their firms. Sam Molinaro, the Chief Financial Officer (CFO) at Bear Stearns before its demise, was described as having "…an accounting background and could hardly be expected to have a view about the firm's growing inventory of exotic securities."[20]

Systemic Risk

Closely related to too-big-to-fail and the problem of moral hazard is that of *systemic risk*. It can be defined as "…the type of risk that has the potential to adversely affect not only a single firm or sector but the economy as a whole."[21] Put simply, if only one bank or financial institution pursues a risky strategy, the financial system as a whole will not be affected if that firm fails. However, if all firms are following similar risky ventures and have become interconnected by purchasing each other's risky financial products, the entire financial sector can come crashing down. This is what happened in the financial crisis of 2008.

The bulk of the systemic risk that built up in the financial sector prior to the collapse in 2008 was due to a financial innovation called *derivatives*, one type of which are credit default swaps (CDSs). These products are called derivatives because they derive their values from a change in the value of the overall market or other financial securities. Derivatives were commonly used in the futures markets for commodities and morphed into financial products in the 1990s. Companies use derivatives to protect themselves against changes in commodity prices or interest rates and their use by speculators provides pricing information to the financial markets.[22]

Derivatives became deadly to the financial markets because of their opaque nature when firms thought that they could use the instruments to insure away all types of risk. The underlying risk in securitized debt was masked and the business community thought that it could pile on mountains of new debt with no risk of bad things happening. Nicole Gelinas, a fellow at the Manhattan Institute and chartered financial analyst, said,

> ...the protection that such derivatives provided made much securitized debt seem nearly riskless. This illusion helped push America's debt levels up nearly 75 percent between 1980 and 2000 relative to gross domestic product, surpassing peaks reached before the Great Depression and increasing at the fastest rate in American history.[23]

Following the burst of the housing bubble in 2006, financial firms not only suffered huge losses on MBSs, but also had to meet obligations incurred due to derivatives contracts that they had issued.

Globalization

The rapid globalization of trade and finance has been a major factor in allowing the US to remain the world's top economy and to enjoy the top spot on the wealth pyramid. A key result of globalization is that financial capital flows freely across borders and is invested in the locations that offer the best yields for the owners of the funds. The American financial markets attract this roving capital and efficiently allocate it to investment opportunities. The reason that globalization worsened the financial crisis is that there is now a global imbalance in savings and spending between the US and other countries; China is the best illustration of this. In the US, the savings rate in the 1970s was 10% and then dropped to -2.5% in 2006. Americans stopped saving and bought cheap Chinese consumer goods; consumer spending accounts for 70% of GDP in the US. In contrast, the savings rate in China was 22% in 2005 and consumer spending made up only 36% of GDP there.[24]

This results in the Chinese being able to rely on sales of exports rather than selling those same goods domestically. The Chinese use the dollars obtained from export sales to purchase US treasury bills and are now the largest holder of US public debt. To rebalance capital flows, China needs to import more and the US needs to save more.

China will find it hard to spur its citizens to save less and spend more until it develops a stronger social safety net that includes comprehensive medical care and a sound retirement system.

Analysis

The ten factors discussed in this paper interacted to cause the greatest financial calamity since the Great Depression. Economists and other experts disagree on which contributing factors had the most impact and there are innumerable opinions on how to proceed in the recovery phase of the Great Recession from which the US is emerging. One thing is certain—the financial landscape has changed and much thought must be brought to bear to forestall another crisis and to shore up the American capitalist system.

Many of the factors that contributed to the financial crisis do not have a direct connection to the Army because it does not have the profit motive of a corporation. The service does not employ financial leverage, does not deal in financial securities, and is only tangentially impacted by the Fed's monetary policy. However, several of the factors can be related to Army operations or have some amount of impact on military business operations.

When the housing bubble burst, many Soldiers lost significant equity in their homes or faced foreclosure because they could not afford higher mortgage payments. Congress approved the Homeowners Assistance Program, which allocated more than $500 million to aid military members affected by declining property values. The Army uses sophisticated models such as the Training Resource Model (TRM) to develop funding requirements. Just as in the financial sector, these models are based on a variety of assumptions and use historical trends to calculate future projections. It is essential that the Army construct carefully the quantitative models that it uses and regularly assess the key assumptions embedded in the design of the models. Finally, the Army must deal daily with the presence of moral hazard, particularly in the areas of weapons procurement and contracting. There are always principle agent problems involved when contractors are responsible for delivering products and services worth tens of billions of dollars. The large number of recent contracting scandals in Iraq and Afghanistan clearly show that more attention needs to be paid to reducing the moral hazard created in Army business operations.

Government Response

The federal government's response to the effects of the financial crisis in America was unprecedented in scale and in scope. First, the Fed began lowering the federal funds rate in September 2007. The rate decreased from 5.25% to 0.25%, essentially reaching zero in December 2008. The Economic Stimulus Act of 2008 was passed by the Bush Administration in February of that year and provided $168 billion in tax rebates. Next, the House of Representatives voted down a Treasury bailout plan in September 2008. A revised version was approved in October as the Emergency Economic Stabilization Act. The legislation created the Troubled Asset Relief Program (TARP) and provided $700 billion to purchase bad assets from banks, mostly MBSs. The Treasury shifted gears and made direct capital investments in financial institutions after it became apparent that the firms were facing insolvency, not a frozen market for the securities on their books.

The Term Asset Loan Facility (TALF) was launched in March 2009 with a goal to "…catalyze the securitization markets"[25] by providing $200 billion of guarantees from the Fed that would stimulate $1 trillion in sales of asset backed securities. At that same time, the American Recovery and Reinvestment Act (ARRA) of 2009 was passed to prove $787 billion in funds to stimulate the economy. The measure included tax cuts, expansion of unemployment benefits, and domestic spending targeted at infrastructure, education, and health care. Numerous other federal initiatives brought the price tag of the government response to well over $2 trillion.

The US Army will be deeply impacted by the recent financial upheaval and must react appropriately to maintain its unparalleled expeditionary and war-fighting capabilities. The primary issues that the Army must be prepared to deal with are the explosion in deficit spending and the national debt and the increasing complexity of its operating environment.

Deficit Spending and the National Debt

The federal government responded to the 2008 financial crisis by spending more than $2 trillion. Private spending by consumers and businesses has taken a nosedive in the past two years and government expenditures served to replace that lost economic activity. This government intervention likely stopped the American economy from continuing a deflationary spiral into depression. The downside is that the financial stimuli have to be financed by borrowing. The crisis response, combined with ongoing legislative initiatives of the Obama Administration, will balloon the national debt to new record levels.

The national debt currently stands at $12 trillion and the Obama Administration projects that it will increase to more than $18 trillion by 2020. It would require more than $800 billion to pay the interest on that amount.[26] The borrowing cost in 2020 would exceed the projected amount to be spent on all discretionary federal programs. The national debt reached $1 trillion in 1981. Since then, it has exploded upward with the greatest annual increases coming between 2000 and the present.

The Danger

The bulging national debt is dangerous for several reasons. First, the interest payments will steadily increase, crowding out investment in defense and other discretionary federal programs. Second, high levels of debt can act as a drag on future economic growth. Recent research by economists Kenneth Rogoff and Carmen Reinhart shows that the growth rates of advanced economies are slowed dramatically when the ratio of total debt to GDP exceeds 90%. Debt-to-GDP is set to pass 90% this year in the US and could exceed 100% by 2012.[27]

Third, there is danger in who is financing America's debt. Foreigners own nearly half of the nation's debt, with the Chinese holding $755 billion in US Treasury bills. The US government must tread carefully in its interactions with China and other foreign governments because it is dependent on them for continued financing. As annual deficits rise, the situation deteriorates further. Comments by foreign officials make it clear that they understand how vulnerable America is in its present financial condition. An official of the Chinese Communist Party commented,

> If the US leader chooses this period to meet the Dalai Lama, that would damage trust and cooperation between our two countries. And how would that help the US surmount the current economic crisis?[28]

Finally, the national debt poses risk because of the approaching crisis in entitlement spending as the *baby boomers* begin to retire. Several administrations have attempted to reform the Social Security and Medicare/Medicaid programs recognizing that current receipts from payroll taxes will soon be less than benefits that must be paid out. No solutions have been found and, in fact, the problem has become more critical as new entitlements such as the prescription drug benefit passed by the Bush Administration were unfunded.[29] If these large entitlement programs are not reformed, budget deficits could increase further adding trillions more to the total debt that must be financed.

A National Security Issue

The dangers just outlined make America's national debt a national security issue. There is a clear connection between the US economy and the security of the nation. A healthy economy enables America to wield all of its instruments of power. President Barack Obama recognized the linkage while addressing the West Point class in December of 2009. He said, "Our prosperity provides a foundation for our power. It pays for our military. It underwrites our diplomacy."[30] There is a growing apprehension that the US is standing at a crossroads due to its deteriorating financial condition. Many economists echo the thoughts of Alan Auerbach of the University of California at Berkeley, who said, "We've moved closer to the precipice, and the precipice has moved closer to us."[31]

There does not seem to be a sense of urgency, however, in the military concerning the ability of the federal government to maintain the present level of discretionary spending. The 2010 Quadrennial Defense Review (QDR) speaks to the challenges brought on by rising economic powers like China and comments on how recent financial crisis makes the operating environment more complex.[32] Likewise, the Army Capstone Concept addresses operations in a world of uncertainty and complexity.[33] The Army Capstone Concept seeks to describe future-armed conflict and how the Army will operate in that new environment. Neither this document nor the QDR points to or alludes to America's financial health as a key to successful military operations in the future.

The health of the US economy must be elevated to a key issue of national security and a top concern for the Army. If the political leadership finds the will to deal with the national debt and the pending crisis in entitlement programs, the impact on Army funding could be significant. A solution that takes the US away from the financial precipice will require tax increases, benefit reductions, and cuts in discretionary spending, including funding for military programs.

Across the board, cuts in discretionary government spending could be significant and might reach 50% or more. Could the Army operate with half as much funding as it receives today? There are alternatives to the current operating environment characterized by worldwide engagement and massive counterinsurgency fights in Iraq and Afghanistan. One option is for US foreign policy to become isolationist in nature, to pull back all armed forces within the nation's borders. This alternative would offer the greatest savings in defense spending. A less radical option is to pursue a military policy like that recently outlined by Bernard Finel, a senior fellow at the American Security Project.

Finel argues against the current effort to transform US forces into one geared toward counterinsurgency operations and extended occupations of other countries. He believes that "…the US should adopt a national military strategy that heavily leverages the core capability to break states and target and destroy fixed assets, iteratively if necessary."[34] Finel's analysis shows that the majority of US military objectives can be achieved early in a campaign and that doing so minimizes the total cost of the effort. Extending operations to long-term occupations only achieves marginal additional objectives while multiplying the total cost many times over. The key here is that there are alternative military strategies that could be chosen, which would permit the defense budget to be reduced sharply in order to contribute to an effort to eliminate deficit spending and pay off a portion of the national debt.

Reforming the System

The Financial Sector

The tragic consequences of the financial crisis of 2008 demand a better way of doing business. The US must reform its financial sector in a way that reduces the systemic risk that large institutions pose to the health of the economy. Financial oversight should control excessive risk taking by limiting financial leverage and increasing transparency of financial information, and should encourage continued creation of innovative financial products while mitigating the risk involved in using those new tools.

In the immediate aftermath of the crisis, there was a strong push for legislation to transform the financial system. The momentum has dissipated and lobbyists for the financial industry have been hard at work pressuring Congress to refrain from legislating major changes. In February 2010, nothing has been done and the opportunity for strengthening the financial sector against future crises is weakening. Comments by Neil Barofsky of the Treasury Department are insightful. He says,

> The problems that led to the crisis have not been addressed, and in some cases have grown worse. Even if TARP saved our financial system from driving off a cliff back in 2008, absent meaningful reform, we are still driving on the same winding mountain road, but this time in a faster car.[35]

Congress is working on a bill, but it is not clear how far it will go in transforming the financial landscape.

The Military

The financial crisis of 2008 has led to calls for transformational changes in the financial sector. The aftermath of the calamity in finance also requires a look into the military to analyze whether changes in its organizations or financial operations are warranted. The US Armed Forces have been "transforming" for years and the use of that word has become a cliché. The Army has moved from a Cold War force designed around divisions to a modular, Brigade Combat Team (BCT)-centric structure. This change is nearly complete and most people are familiar with BCTs since these organizational structures are the basis for the combat rotations into Iraq and Afghanistan.

The Army is now working to craft an operating strategy to utilize the new BCT structure in the future security environment. That strategy is detailed in the Army Capstone Concept (ACC), known as the Training and Doctrine Command (TRADOC) Pamphlet 525-3-0. Published in December 2009, this document outlines the key idea of *operational adaptability*. The Army plans to operate in an environment of increasing complexity and uncertainty and to do so under conditions of continual conflict until at least 2028. The QDR released in February 2010 provides a further window into the conditions expected in the future security environment and lists changes required in the military forces to permit successful combat operations to occur in the years ahead.

The core idea of operational adaptability requires leaders and organizations to demonstrate a quality "…based on critical thinking, comfort with ambiguity and decentralization, a willingness to accept prudent risk, and an ability to make rapid adjustments based on a continuous assessment of the situation."[36] In the foreword to the ACC, General Martin Dempsey of TRADOC calls for leaders "…who are comfortable with collaborative planning and decentralized execution" and to "be prepared to decentralize operations."[37] *Decentralization* is a critical organizational requirement called for in the ACC. According to the Army's new Leadership Development Strategy, one of three paradigm shifts occurring in the operational environment is "the effect of decentralization."[38] Decentralization requires that decision making and responsibility be pushed to the lowest levels within an organization. The Leadership Development Strategy describes how the Army will develop future leaders who can handle the increased burden of responsibility.

The Army is a very large, centralized bureaucracy; so it would seem that the organization is being asked to turn itself inside out. Two entrepreneurs have a few good suggestions in a recent book entitled *The Starfish and the Spider*. Ori Brafman and Rod Beckstrom describe *spiders* as those organizations (e.g., the Army) that are bureaucratic and inflexible, vulnerable to defeat as their legs are cut off one by one. *Starfish* organizations (e.g., Al Qaeda) are decentralized and regenerate themselves if an arm is cut off. The authors comment that, "…when attacked, decentralized organizations become even more decentralized…when attacked, centralized organizations tend to become even more centralized."[39]

The authors suggest three ways that spiders can win out over the starfish. First, one can attempt to change the ideology of the starfish organization. This is extremely difficult to do. Second, the decentralized starfish organization can be forced to centralize. This is hard to do also. These strategies both rely on "…changing or reducing the power and effectiveness of decentralized systems," so the third option is to make the bureaucratic spider organization into one that is more decentralized. Brafman and

Beckstrom think that decentralizing portions of the centralized organization to create *The Hybrid Organization* is the most feasible route to follow. They point to companies like eBay, Amazon, Intuit, and Google that followed various strategies to decentralize parts of their otherwise centralized organizations.[40]

While parts of the Army organization could be seen as decentralized—notably Special Operations units—most of the service is a highly centralized bureaucracy. The Army financial management community is a small part of the force structure, but its operations are particularly centralized and have become more so in the past decade. The Army's financial operations rely extensively on contractor maintained computer models to develop funding requirements having moved away from *bottom-up* methods that were used in the past. Budget execution is often controlled from and key spending decisions made at headquarters two or more levels above the organization where the rubber meets the road. Compounding this problem is the fact that Army operating funds are strictly divided into many different spending categories, limiting flexibility. Lieutenant Colonel (Retired) Mick Simonelli describes his experience spending funds after 9/11 to build the Afghanistan National Army. He said,

> Many of the funding problems were rooted in the dysfunctional budget categories that our stateside Headquarters had given us. Washington and Central Command had placed unrealistic restrictions on the funds…I did everything I could to support the Army financially. I only had two choices: break the financial rules and keep the new Army alive, or enforce the rules and let the Army die.[41]

The financial community, like most other sectors of the Army, needs to explore ways to decentralize how it does business and generate more agility to respond to a complex, uncertain operating environment. As Congress debates legislation to reform the commercial world of American finance, it is imperative that Army financial leaders use the present opportunity to implement reforms that will ensure robust support to Soldiers engaged in continual conflict. A few ideas for reform are proposed below.

Recommendations

Financial Contingency Plans

Army financial planners have been expecting that the rapid rise in funding levels since 9/11 would end and that Army financial resources would decline as commitments in Iraq and other places subsided. The Obama Administration announced in January 2010 that it would increase the Pentagon budget by $100 billion over the period 2011–2015 to pay for increased personnel and equipment costs.[42] Thus, it seems likely that cuts in Army funding might not come until the middle of this decade.

If the federal government properly prioritizes the runaway budget deficits and unprecedented increase in the national debt as a top national security issue, discretionary spending will have to be cut. The Army financial community should, therefore, develop financial contingency plans that specify how to achieve budget cuts of 10–50%. Once developed, these plans can be updated annually and kept on the shelf just as operational war plans are.

The Common Levels of Support (CLS) framework used by Army Installation Management Command (IMCOM) is an example of a tool that provides financial management capability to assess the impact of reduced funding levels. The CLS program assigns a Capability Level (CL) to each subcomponent of a service provided on an Army installation. Ratings are coded green, amber, red, and black based on the funding available to provide the service. If 100% of the required funding is allocated, the rating would be CL-1 or green indicating that there is no risk in being able to fully provide the service capability to all customers.[43] Lower ratings result if less financial resources are made available; thus, IMCOM financial managers can clearly show how declining dollars map to reduced service levels. Other Army organizations need to deploy financial management tools that permit analysts to easily portray and manage the effects of funding reductions.

The Army should shift financial planning expertise from other activities to provide the manpower required to develop financial contingency plans. Currently, Army financial experts spend a great deal of time drafting and maintaining *unresourced requirement* (URR) lists. These lists outline requirements that are unfunded in the budget, but could be resourced if additional dollars appeared. In today's resourced constrained environment, maintaining URR lists is a wasted endeavor. The financial planning effort should be redirected to crafting plans to deal with deep budget cuts that are more likely every day.

Army Financial Reform

The financial crisis of 2008 makes clear the necessity for America to overhaul and restructure its financial system. Similarly, the Army needs to immediately reorganize its financial tool kit, decentralize its financial processes and operations, and alter how it trains and rewards its financial workforce. These changes will allow the financial arm of the Army to generate the "operational adaptability" called for in the ACC and to apply financial agility in a coming era of declining budgets.

The Army financial community has recognized for years that its financial automation network is a dinosaur. Thousands of separate systems that are not integrated and cannot share information prevent the effective pooling of financial data into reports that leaders can use to make decisions. The Department of Defense (DoD) is one of the only federal departments still unable to get a clean audit of its annual financial statements – each of its components shares a portion of the blame. The Army is in the midst of fielding a commercial off-the-shelf (COTS) Enterprise Resource Planning (ERP) suite of software. The service is calling the implementation of the SAP software the General Fund Enterprise Business System (GFEBS) and the conversion to this platform will completely revamp how the Army runs its finances.

The Army must get this implementation right the first time, but the difficulties loom large. Other software initiatives demonstrate the tough road ahead. The DoD cancelled the Defense Integrated Military Human Resources System (DIMHRS) in February 2010 after years of effort and a billion dollars had been spent. The software would have integrated more than 90 personnel and pay management systems currently in use.[44] The Army has had challenges in completing much smaller software implementations for travel planning, automation of receipt documents, and supply and financial system interface.

Assuming that GFEBS works, the Army must immediately bring to bear the power of the ERP solution to seamlessly pass financial information from its lowest organizations to the decision makers at Department of the Army (DA). The main reason for the wholesale replacement of the Army's financial infrastructure is to solve the problem of not being able to extract financial data from the current web of automation systems. One of the main reasons justifying the centralization of financial operations in the Army has been that senior decision makers cannot wait for data to filter up through the layers of the present system. Effective use of the new ERP tools should allow most financial processes to be decentralized to a much lower level while increasing the availability of financial intelligence to commanders and senior managers. This will permit more agile support to Soldiers at ground level and improve the decision-making ability of their leaders.

The Army can further increase its financial flexibility by moving away from the use of one-year appropriations. Currently, most types of funds are only authorized for one year and must be spent by September 30th—the last day of the fiscal year. The Army should work with the DoD Comptroller and Congress to move most appropriations to a two-year basis to align with the biennial budget process that was implemented in the 1980s. A reasonable control mechanism would be to require 80% of an appropriation to be obligated in the first year and allow 20% of the funding to cross the fiscal year boundary to be spent in year two. This change would lessen the frantic effort to spend 100% of one-year funding by the last day of the fiscal year and could offer Army organizations more flexibility in the years when the appropriations bill is not passed in time to start the new fiscal year on October 1st.

The third aspect of revamping the Army financial environment is improving the pool of human capital. The revolutionary potential of GFEBS will not be realized unless the financial community expands the capabilities of its employees. Commanders rely on budget analysts, accountants, and auditors to meticulously watch the books, but these team members are not often associated with break through ideas or exciting new ways of doing business. This must change in the times of uncertainty that lie ahead.

The DoD Comptroller, the Honorable Robert F. Hale, recently summarized his thoughts on what he wants the financial workforce to emphasize. He said,

> I have asked Defense financial managers to do three things as we go forward: Work hard but smart, especially by setting priorities. Search for efficiencies. Even small ones can add up. And focus on training and professional development, including new approaches.[45]

The Army must demand more of its financial workforce and should offer the employees more opportunities to learn new skills. First, employees seeking to move above the GS-12 equivalent level or the rank of Major should be required to obtain one or more professional certifications. The two most common are the Certified Defense Financial Manager (CDFM) and the Certified Government Financial Manager (CGFM). Other certifications are available in many financial specialties. Second, those same employees should be required to have a Masters Degree in a financial discipline in order to advance. Third, financial experts at the GS-15 equivalent level or rank of Colonel should be required to submit an article for publication at least once every two years. An employee that meets these goals demonstrates a high level of initiative and is likely to be one that can contribute significantly to his or her organization.

The Army, in turn, must expand training opportunities and incentives offered to its financial workforce. The service could expand the opportunities to attend the Defense Comptrollership Program at Syracuse University or other education programs that confer a graduate degree in a financial field. Financial or advancement incentives could be offered to employees that achieve one or more professional certifications. The Army currently recruits college graduates into its intern program. The financial community should also target for hiring civilians that have two to five years experience in the commercial financial sector particularly those that have worked with ERP solutions. This practical experience could prove vital as the GFEBS implementation concludes and the Army looks to maximize the benefit from the new suite of software. Finally, the Army must develop a civilian performance evaluation system that ties pay to performance so that it can reward and advance the most capable employees. The National Security Personnel System (NSPS) was being implemented across DoD to achieve this goal, but the National Defense Authorization Act of 2010 included a provision ending this pay-for-performance system after only a few years of use.[46]

Educate the Workforce

One of the most severe consequences of the financial crisis is the impact on the individual consumer. The average middle class family suffered significant losses on retirement accounts and other investments and millions saw their mortgages go into foreclosure or lost significant equity in their homes as the housing bubble burst. As an employer, the Army is one of the largest "corporations," having well over one million employees including Soldiers, DA civilians, and contractors.

The Army needs to aggressively invest in educating its workforce in matters of personal finance. The service currently offers training and assistance on a voluntary basis through Army Community Service (ACS) offices on most military installations. Training should be mandatory and be programmed into all professional development courses. Employees that are financially astute will be better prepared to withstand the effects of future financial downturns. They will provide more consistent effort to the Army if they are not distracted due to personal financial challenges at home. Deploying Soldiers will have one less thing to worry about while serving on combat tours if they have sound personal finances.

One way for the Army to provide the education in personal finance would be to partner with a commercial financial institution such as United Services Automobile Association (USAA) or other firms that offer comprehensive financial services. Founded in 1922 by a group of Army officers, USAA is a fully integrated financial services company that serves more than seven million members of the military. A partnership between the Army and a firm like this could offer a system of life-long financial education that would provide Army employees with the tools necessary to make informed decisions on investments, home purchases, insurance, and other key financial issues.

The investment necessary to implement a broad-based education program in personal financial management would pay for itself in a short time. Financially savvy employees will have greater productivity and will need to take less time off to deal with financial emergencies. In today's volatile financial environment, the Army needs to provide this employment benefit to all of its members.

Conclusion

The financial crisis of 2008 and the resulting Great Recession have tested the American system of capitalism. While the initial signs of recovery are evident, problems persist. The housing market is shaky, with home sales falling 11% in January 2010 to the lowest level since record keeping began in 1963.[47] The unemployment rate is still at 9.7% and not projected to decrease much in the next two years. Credit remains tight, particularly for small businesses. Core consumer prices fell in January 2010 by 0.1%, the first decline since 1982, raising new fears that deflation might still come to grip the US economy. Deflation is particularly worrisome because industry is only operating at 72% of capacity, far below the monthly average since 1967 of 81%.[48]

The recent financial upheaval has impacted the Army and will continue to affect the service and its financial operations far into the future. The uncontrolled deficit spending initiated in response to the credit crisis will double or triple the national debt in the next ten years. A determined government response to this threat to US national security will necessitate cuts in discretionary federal spending leading to a loss of funding for the Army in the coming decade.

The Army can position itself for success by taking seriously the recommendations offered in this paper. It should develop financial contingency plans to blunt the effect of budget cuts, commit itself to financial reforms that enable more decentralized financial processes, and implement a training program for its workforce that arms each employee with the knowledge and tools to create a robust personal financial plan. The measures will permit the Army to thrive in a future environment of uncertainty.

BIBLIOGRAPHY

"A Leader Development Strategy for a 21st Century Army." Department of the Army, November 25, 2009.

Acharya, Viral V. and Matthew Richardson, eds. *Restoring Financial Stability: How to Repair a Failed System.* Hoboken, NJ: John Wiley & Sons, Inc., 2009.

Barbera, Robert J. *The Cost of Capitalism: Understanding Market Mayhem and Stabilizing Our Economic Future.* New York: McGraw Hill, 2009.

Beck, Glenn. *Glenn Beck's Common Sense: The Case Against an Out-of-control Government, Inspired by Thomas Paine.* New York: Mercury Radio Arts/Threshold Editions, 2009.

Bergsten, C. Fred. "The Dollar and the Deficits: How Washington Can Prevent the Next Crisis." *Foreign Affairs* 88, no. 6 (November/December 2009): 20–38.

Blustein, Paul. *Misadventures of the Most Favored Nations.* New York: Public Affairs, 2009.

Boskin, Michael J. "When Deficits Become Dangerous." *The Wall Street Journal*, February 12, 2010, A23.

Brafman, Ori and Rod A. Beckstrom. *The Starfish and the Spider: The Unstoppable Power of Leaderless Organizations.* New York: Penguin Group, 2006.

Chandler, Marc. *Making Sense of the Dollar: Exposing Dangerous Myths about Trade and Foreign Exchange.* New York: Bloomburg Press, 2009.

Ciorciari, John D. and John B. Taylor, eds. *The Road Ahead for the Fed.* Stanford, CA: Hoover Institution Press, 2009.

Cohan, William. D. *House of Cards: A Tale of Hubris and Wretched Excess on Wall Street.* New York: Doubleday Publishing Group, 2009.

Coy, Peter. "US Debt: It's Not Dark Yet, but it's Getting There." *Bloomberg Business Week*, February 15, 2010, 16.

Dodaro, Gene L. "Maximizing DOD's Potential to Face New Fiscal Challenges and Strengthen Interagency Partnerships." Presentation to the National Defense University, Washington, DC, January 6, 2010, online URL http://www.gao.gov/products/GAO-10-359CG.

Enthoven, Alain C. and K. Wayne Smith. *How Much is Enough? Shaping the Defense Program 1961-1969.* Santa Monica, CA: Rand Corporation, 2005.

Feldstein, Martin. "How Obama Should Shrink *His* Deficit." *The Wall Street Journal*, February 19, 2010, A13.

Finel, Bernard I. "An Alternative to COIN: It's time to adapt our security strategy to leverage America's conventional strengths." *Armed Forces Journal*, February 2010, 22–27 and 36–37.

Friedberg, Aaron L. *The Weary Titan: Britain and the Experience of Relative Decline 1895–1905*. Princeton, NJ: Princeton University Press, 1988.

Gasparino, Charles. *The Sellout: How Three Decades of Wall Street Greed and Government Mismanagement Destroyed the Global Financial System*. New York: Harper Collins, 2009.

Gelinas, Nicole. *After the Fall: Saving Capitalism from Wall Street and Washington*. New York: Encounter Books, 2009.

Goldberg, Matthew S. "Long-Term Implications of the Department of Defense's Fiscal Year 2010 Budget Submission." Testimony before the Committee on Armed Services, US House of Representatives, November 18, 2009, online URL http://www.cbo.gov/ftpdocs/107xx/doc10730/11-18-FY2010_DoD_Budget.pdf.

Hale, Robert F. "Three Challenges for Defense Financial Managers." *Armed Forces Comptroller* 54, no. 4 (Fall 2009): 8–11.

Holtz-Eakin, Douglas. "The Coming Deficit Disaster." *The Wall Street Journal*, November 21–22, 2009, A15.

Kauffman, Henry. *The Road to Financial Reformation: Warnings, Consequences, Reforms*. Hoboken, NJ: John Wiley & Sons, Inc., 2009.

Korb, Lawrence and Laura Conley. "Blueprint for Defense Transformation." *The American Interest*, September/October 2009, 64–72.

Maurer, Harry and Cristina Lindblad, eds. "The Week in Business: Economics & Policy." *Bloomburg BusinessWeek*, March 8, 2010, 6.

Miller, Rich. "Why the 'D' Word is Back on the Table." *Bloomburg BusinessWeek*, March 8, 2010, 16.

Morris, Charles R. *The Two Trillion Dollar Meltdown: Easy Money, High Rollers, and the Great Credit Crash*. New York: Public Affairs, 2008.

Muolo, Paul. *$700 Billion Bailout: The Emergency Economic Stabilization Act and What it Means to You, Your Money, Your Mortgage, and Your Taxes*. Hoboken, NJ: John Wiley & Sons, Inc., 2009.

Muradian, Vago. "White House to add $100B to 5-year defense budget plan." *Army Times*, January 11, 2010, 12.

O'Hanlon, Michael E. *Budgeting for Hard Power: Defense and Security Spending Under Barrack Obama*. Washington, DC: Brookings Institution Press, 2009.

Ottinger, Maurice A. "Measuring Service Performance at Army Installations." *Armed Forces Comptroller* 54, no. 1 (Winter 2009): 26–9.

Phillips, Kevin. *Bad Money: Reckless Finance, Failed Politics, and the Global Crisis of American Capitalism.* New York: Penguin Group, 2008.

Philpott, Tom. "DIMHRS program dumped as 'a disaster'." *Stars and Stripes*, February 20, 2010, online URL http://www.stripes.com/article.asp?section=125&article=68142.

Posner, Richard A. *A Failure of Capitalism: The Crisis of '08 and the Descent into Depression.* Cambridge, MA: Harvard University Press, 2009.

Pozen, Robert. *Too Big to Save?: How to Fix the US Financial System.* Hoboken, NJ: John Wiley & Sons, Inc., 2010.

Reinhart, Carmen M. and Kenneth S. Rogoff. *This Time is Different: Eight Centuries of Financial Folly.* Princeton, NJ: Princeton University Press, 2009.

"Quadrennial Defense Review Report." Department of Defense, February 2010.

Sapolsky, Harvey M., Eugene Gholz, and Caitlin Talmadge. *US Defense Politics: The Origins of Security Policy*. New York: Routledge, 2009.

Shelton, Judy. "The US: Debtor and Leader?" *The Wall Street Journal*, February 17, 2010, A15.

Shiller, Robert J. *The Subprime Solution: How Today's Global Financial Crisis Happened, and What to do About It.* Princeton, NJ: Princeton University Press, 2008.

Simonelli, Mick. *Riding a Donkey Backwards Through Afghanistan: How I Successfully Spent $400 Million of Your Taxpayer Dollars to Build the Afghanistan National Army.* Minneapolis, MN: Mill City Press, 2009.

Spratt, John and Hugh Brady. "National Security vs. Social Security: Is the Defense Budget Sustainable?" *The Brookings Review* 20, no. 3 (Summer 2002): 8-12.

Taylor, John B. *Getting Off Track: How Government Actions and Interventions Caused, Prolonged, and Worsened the Financial Crisis.* Stanford, CA: Hoover Institution Press, 2009.

"The Army Capstone Concept." Department of the Army, December 21, 2009.

"The Welfare State and Military Power." *The Wall Street Journal*, December 4, 2009, A24.

Wagner, Daniel and Alan Zibel. "Inspector for bailout says finance system may fail again," *Austin American Statesman*, January 31, 2010, A2.

Weigelt, Matthew and Doug Beizer. "As NSPS ends, employees wait for what's next." *Federal Computer Week*, October 30, 2009, online URL http://fcw.com/articles/2009/10/30/nsps-end-wait-for-next-step.aspx.

Weisman, Jonathan. "Deficit to Hit All-Time High." *The Wall Street Journal*, February 1, 2010, A1.

Wessel, David. *In Fed We Trust: Ben Bernanke's War on the Great Panic.* New York: Crown Business, 2009.

Whitehouse, Mark. "Deficit, Budget Woes Need Solutions as US Nears the Precipice." *The Wall Street Journal*, January 4, 2010, A2.

Woods, Thomas E., Jr. *Meltdown: A Free-market Look at Why the Stock Market Collapsed, the Economy Tanked, and Government Bailouts Will Make Things Worse.* Washington, DC: Regnery Publishing, Inc., 2009.

Zakheim, Dov S. "Security Challenges Arising from the Global Economic Crisis." Statement Before the House Committee on Armed Services, March 11, 2009, online URL http://www.fpri.org/enotes/200903.zakheim.securityeconomiccrisis.html.

ENDNOTES

[1] John Taylor, *Getting Off Track*, (Stanford, CA: Hoover Institution Press, 2009), 2–3.

[2] David Wessel, "Bernanke's Puzzling Bubble Logic," *The Wall Street Journal*, January 14, 2010, A2.

[3] Robert Shiller, *The Subprime Solution*, (Princeton, NJ: Princeton University Press, 2008), 32–5.

[4] Thomas Woods, Jr., *Meltdown*, (Washington, DC: Regnery Publishing, Inc., 2009), 13–4.

[5] Thomas Woods, Jr., *Meltdown*, (Washington, DC: Regnery Publishing, Inc., 2009), 17–8.

[6] Charles Morris, *The Two Trillion Dollar Meltdown*, (New York: PublicAffairs, 2008), xvii.

[7] Viral Acharya and Matthew Richardson, eds., *Restoring Financial Stability*, (New York: John Wiley & Sons, Inc., 2009), 63.

[8] Viral Acharya and Matthew Richardson, eds., *Restoring Financial Stability*, (New York: John Wiley & Sons, Inc., 2009), 64.

[9] Robert Pozen, *Too Big to Save?* (New York: John Wiley & Sons, Inc., 2010), 73.

[10] Robert Pozen, *Too Big to Save?* (New York: John Wiley & Sons, Inc., 2010), 69–71.

[11] Robert Pozen, *Too Big to Save?* (New York: John Wiley & Sons, Inc., 2010), 83–92.

[12] Robert Pozen, *Too Big to Save?* (New York: John Wiley & Sons, Inc., 2010), 58–9.

[13] Henry Kauffman, *The Road to Financial Reformation*, (New York: John Wiley & Sons, Inc., 2009), 39–40.

[14] Thomas Woods, Jr., *Meltdown*, (Washington, DC: Regnery Publishing, Inc., 2009), 47.

[15] Nicole Gelinas, *After the Fall*, (New York: Encounter Books, 2009), 86–7.

[16] Richard Posner, *A Failure of Capitalism*, (Cambridge, MA: Harvard University Press, 2009), 26–7.

[17] Robert Barbera, *The Cost of Capitalism*, (New York: McGraw Hill, 2009), 49.

[18] David Wessel, *In Fed We Trust*, (New York: Crown Business, 2009), 174.

[19] Nicole Gelinas, *After the Fall*, (New York: Encounter Books, 2009), 43–9.

[20] William Cohan, *House of Cards*, (New York: Doubleday Publishing, 2009), 291.

[21] John Ciorciari and John Taylor, eds. *The Road Ahead for the Fed*, (Stanford, CA: Hoover Institution Press, 2009), 151.

[22] Nicole Gelinas, *After the Fall*, (New York: Encounter Books, 2009), 84–5.

[23] Nicole Gelinas, *After the Fall*, (New York: Encounter Books, 2009), 97.

[24] Robert Pozen, *Too Big to Save?* (New York: John Wiley & Sons, Inc., 2010), 324–6.

[25] John Ciorciari and John Taylor, eds. *The Road Ahead for the Fed*, (Stanford, CA: Hoover Institution Press, 2009), 76.

[26] Martin Feldstein, "How Obama Should Shrink *His* Deficit," *The Wall Street Journal*, February 19, 2010, A13.

[27] Peter Coy, "US Debt: It's not Dark Yet, But it's Getting There," *Bloomburg BusinessWeek*, February 15, 2010, 16.

[28] Judy Shelton, "The United States: Debtor and Leader?," *The Wall Street Journal*, February 17, 2010, A15.

[29] Michael Boskin, "When Deficits Become Dangerous," *The Wall Street Journal*, February 12, 2010, A23.

[30] "The Welfare State and Military Power," *The Wall Street Journal*, December 4, 2009, A24.

[31] Mark Whitehouse, "Deficit, Budget Woes Need Solutions as US Nears the Precipice," *The Wall Street Journal*, January 4, 2010, A2.

[32] "Quadrennial Defense Review Report." Department of Defense, February 2010, 7.

[33] "The Army Capstone Concept," Department of the Army, December 21, 2009, 7-8.

[34] Bernard Finel, "An Alternative to COIN: It's time to adapt our security strategy to leverage America's conventional strengths," *Armed Forces Journal*, February 2010, 23.

[35] Daniel Wagner and Alan Zibel, "Inspector for bailout says finance system may fail again," *Austin American-Statesman*, January 31, 2010, A2.

[36] "The Army Capstone Concept," Department of the Army, December 21, 2009, 16.

[37] "The Army Capstone Concept," Department of the Army, December 21, 2009, i–ii.

[38] " A Leader Development Strategy for a 21st Century Army," Department of the Army, 3–4.

[39] Ori Brafman and Rod Beckstrom, *The Starfish and the Spider*, (New York: Penguin Group, 2006), 139.

[40] Ori Brafman and Rod Beckstrom, *The Starfish and the Spider*, (New York: Penguin Group, 2006), 161–178.

[41] Mick Simonelli, *Riding a Donkey Backwards Through Afghanistan*, (Minneapolis, MN: Mill City Press, Inc., 2009), 81 and 90.

[42] Vago Muradian, "White House to add $100B to 5-year defense budget plan," *Army Times*, January 11, 2010, 12.

[43] Maurice Ottinger, "Measuring Service Performance at Army Installations," *Armed Forces Comptroller*, Winter 2009, 26–7.

[44] Tom Philpott, "DIMHRS program dumped as 'a disaster'," *Stars and Stripes*, February 20, 2010, online URL http://www.stripes.com/article.asp?section=125&article=68142.

[45] Robert Hale, "Three Challenges for Defense Financial Managers,' *Armed Forces Comptroller*, Fall 2009, 11.

[46] Matthew Weigelt and Doug Beizer, "As NSPS ends, employees wait for what's next," *Federal Computer Week*, October 30, 2009, online URL http://fcw.com/articles/2009/10/30/nsps-end-wait-for-next-step.aspx.

[47] Harry Maurer and Cristina Lindblad, eds., "The Week in Business: Economics & Policy," *Bloomburg BusinessWeek*, March 8, 2010, 6.

[48] Rich Miller, "Why the 'D' Word is Back on the Table," *Bloomburg BusinessWeek*, March 8, 2010, 16.